WORKBOOK

For

Your Brain on Art

How the Arts Transform Us

[A Guide To Implementing Susan Magsamen's Book]

Kelly Press

Table of Content

How To Use This Workbook

This workbook provides you with the chance to investigate a variety of aspects of your life, identify areas in need of improvement, and observe your advancement. It has a compilation of essential topics, questions to stimulate contemplation, and learning review questions to gauge your progression.

To ensure you stay on track and make progress, it's advised that you establish a timeline for completing the workbook. Set aside specific periods to work through the prompts and learning review questions. This will help you maintain your momentum and ensure you make steady progress.

The workbook commences with a short recap of the main book, acquainting you with the topic discussed in the title. This approach is highly beneficial for obtaining a deeper understanding of the content covered in the workbook, as well as identifying the areas that require the most attention.

The key lessons and the action prompts provided in this workbook aim to inspire contemplation on various facets of your life. You need not respond to all of them simultaneously and may revisit them later. They serve as a base for your self-reflection and personal exploration.

Once you complete the activities in this workbook, you can assess your progress by answering self-assessment questions. The purpose of these questions is to prompt you to reflect on your learning and identify which areas you need to focus on more. Armed with this knowledge, you can devise effective strategies to enhance your comprehension of the material.

Feel free to spend enough time on the prompts and self-assessment questions. You do not need to finish them in one go. You can take a pause and come back to them later. The most significant thing is to be truthful to yourself and to give careful thought to your responses.

Good luck!

Kelly Press

Overview

Your Brain on Art: How the Arts Transform Us is a book written by Susan Magsamen that explores the transformative power of art on the human brain and its impact on our overall well-being.

The book is divided into two main parts. In the first part, Magsamen discusses the scientific research and studies that have been conducted on the effects of art on the brain. She explains how different forms of art, such as music, visual art, and dance, can activate different parts of the brain and trigger various emotional responses. She also explores how engaging with art can enhance our creativity, empathy, and critical thinking skills, as well as improve our physical and mental health.

In the second part of the book, Magsamen delves into practical applications of art in our daily lives. She suggests ways to incorporate art into our routines, such as listening to music during our commute, visiting museums and art galleries, and engaging in creative activities like drawing, painting, or writing. She also provides examples of how art is being used in healthcare, education, and other fields to improve outcomes for patients and students.

Throughout the book, Magsamen emphasizes the importance of experiencing and creating art as a means of self-expression and personal growth. She argues that art has the power to connect us to our emotions, our communities, and our world in a way that few other activities can.

Your Brain on Art is a compelling and informative read that highlights the transformative power of art on the human brain and its potential to enhance our lives in meaningful ways.

The Anatomy of the Arts

Key Lessons

1. The arts engage multiple parts of the brain: Engaging in the arts activates various parts of the brain, including those responsible for perception, emotion, and cognitive processing.

2. Art can enhance empathy and understanding: The arts can help us understand and relate to different perspectives and experiences, promoting empathy and compassion.

3. Creating art can be therapeutic: Engaging in the creative process can have therapeutic benefits, helping to reduce stress and anxiety, increase positive emotions, and improve overall well-being.

4. Exposure to art can improve cognitive function: Viewing and experiencing art can enhance cognitive functions such as attention, memory, and problem-solving skills.

5. The arts can promote social connection: Participating in or experiencing the arts can create opportunities for social connection and community building, helping to foster a sense of belonging and support.

Action Prompts

How do you typically engage with the arts, and how might you expand your artistic experiences to engage different parts of your brain?

_____

_____

_____

_____

_____

_____

_____

_____

_____

_____

_____

_____

_____

Have you ever experienced a moment of increased empathy or understanding through engaging with art? What was it about the artwork that facilitated this connection?

_____

_____

_____

_____

_____

_____

_____

_____

_____

_____

_____

_____

_____

In what ways might you incorporate creative practices into your daily life to promote therapeutic benefits and improve your overall well-being?

_____

_____

_____

_____

_____

_____

_____

_____

_____

_____

_____

_____

_____

_____

How might you integrate more opportunities to view or experience art into your daily routine to enhance cognitive function and promote brain health?

_____

_____

_____

_____

_____

_____

_____

_____

_____

_____

_____

_____

_____

_____

Have you ever felt a sense of connection or belonging through participating in the arts? What was it about the experience that made you feel connected?

_____

_____

_____

_____

_____

_____

_____

_____

_____

_____

_____

_____

_____

How might you use art to explore and express your emotions in a healthy and productive way?

_____

_____

_____

_____

_____

_____

_____

_____

_____

_____

_____

_____

_____

_____

_____

In what ways might you encourage others in your community to engage with the arts and experience the benefits of social connection and community building?

_____

_____

_____

_____

_____

_____

_____

_____

_____

_____

_____

_____

_____

What is one new artistic experience you could try this week to engage your brain, promote well-being, or foster social connection?

_____

_____

_____

_____

_____

_____

_____

_____

_____

_____

_____

_____

_____

Cultivating Well-Being

Key Lessons

1. Art can be a powerful tool for promoting mental health and well-being. Studies have shown that engaging in artistic activities can help reduce symptoms of anxiety, depression, and stress.

2. Experiencing art can activate the reward center in the brain, leading to feelings of pleasure and satisfaction. This can be particularly helpful for individuals who struggle with addiction or other mental health issues.

3. Art can also help individuals build resilience by promoting a sense of purpose, fostering a positive attitude, and providing opportunities for social connection.

4. Engaging in creative pursuits can improve cognitive function, including memory, attention, and problem-solving abilities. This can be especially beneficial for older adults or individuals with neurodegenerative disorders.

5. Participating in the arts can promote a sense of personal growth and fulfillment. Whether through creating, experiencing, or appreciating art, individuals can develop a greater understanding of themselves and the world around them.

Action Prompts

How do you currently incorporate art into your daily life, and how might you increase your engagement with creative pursuits?

_____

_____

_____

_____

_____

_____

_____

_____

_____

_____

_____

_____

_____

_____

In what ways do you feel that art has helped you manage stress or difficult emotions in the past?

_____

_____

_____

_____

_____

_____

_____

_____

_____

_____

_____

_____

_____

_____

How might you use art as a tool to promote greater well-being and resilience in your life?

_____

_____

_____

_____

_____

_____

_____

_____

_____

_____

_____

_____

_____

What types of artistic activities do you find most
rewarding, and how might you prioritize these activities
in your schedule?

_____

_____

_____

_____

_____

_____

_____

_____

_____

_____

_____

_____

_____

How has your relationship with art evolved over time,
and what lessons have you learned from this evolution?

_____

_____

_____

_____

_____

_____

_____

_____

_____

_____

_____

_____

_____

_____

What barriers do you face in engaging with the arts, and
how might you overcome these challenges?

_____

_____

_____

_____

_____

_____

_____

_____

_____

_____

_____

_____

_____

_____

How can you use art to connect with others and build a
sense of community or social support?

_____

_____

_____

_____

_____

_____

_____

_____

_____

_____

_____

_____

What goals do you have for your artistic practice, and how can you work towards achieving these goals in a meaningful and sustainable way?

_____

_____

_____

_____

_____

_____

_____

_____

_____

_____

_____

_____

_____

_____

Restoring Mental Health

Key Lessons

1. The arts can help reduce stress and anxiety: Engaging in creative activities such as painting, drawing, or music can help calm the mind and reduce stress and anxiety levels.

2. Art can promote emotional regulation: By engaging in creative activities, you can learn to regulate your emotions and become more self-aware of your feelings.

3. Art can help build resilience: Creating art can be a therapeutic way to process difficult experiences and build resilience.

4. Art can improve cognitive function: Engaging in creative activities can improve cognitive function, including memory, attention, and problem-solving skills.

5. Art can promote social connectedness: Participating in artistic activities can help you connect with others and build a sense of community.

Action Prompts

How often do you engage in creative activities, and how do these activities make you feel?

_____

_____

_____

_____

_____

_____

_____

_____

_____

_____

_____

_____

What are some creative activities that you've always wanted to try, but haven't yet? What's holding you back?

_____

_____

_____

_____

_____

_____

_____

_____

_____

_____

_____

_____

_____

_____

_____

How do you typically cope with stress and anxiety?
Could incorporating more artistic activities into your life
help you manage these feelings?

_____

_____

_____

_____

_____

_____

_____

_____

_____

_____

_____

_____

_____

_____

Are there any difficult experiences that you could explore through art? How might creating art help you process and work through these experiences?

_____

_____

_____

_____

_____

_____

_____

_____

_____

_____

_____

_____

_____

How do you typically regulate your emotions? Could incorporating creative activities help you develop new strategies for emotional regulation?

_____

_____

_____

_____

_____

_____

_____

_____

_____

_____

_____

_____

_____

In what ways do you currently connect with others? Could you incorporate more artistic activities into your social life to promote connectedness?

_____

_____

_____

_____

_____

_____

_____

_____

_____

_____

_____

_____

_____

_____

Are there any cognitive skills that you would like to improve? Could engaging in creative activities help you achieve these goals?

_____

_____

_____

_____

_____

_____

_____

_____

_____

_____

_____

_____

_____

_____

_____

How might you incorporate more artistic activities into your daily routine, even if you have a busy schedule?

_____

_____

_____

_____

_____

_____

_____

_____

_____

_____

_____

_____

Healing the Body

Key Lessons

1. Art can help reduce stress and promote relaxation: Engaging in creative activities such as painting, drawing, or writing can help lower levels of the stress hormone cortisol and promote feelings of calm and relaxation.

2. Art can promote physical healing: Studies have shown that viewing art or participating in creative activities can help reduce pain, anxiety, and other symptoms in patients with chronic illnesses.

3. Music can have therapeutic benefits: Music has been shown to help improve mood, reduce anxiety, and even lower blood pressure in people with hypertension.

4. Movement and dance can improve physical and mental well-being: Participating in dance or movement-based activities can improve flexibility, strength, balance, and coordination, as well as boost mood and reduce stress.

5. Art can promote self-expression and personal growth: Engaging in creative activities can help people explore their thoughts, feelings, and

experiences, leading to greater self-awareness, self-confidence, and personal growth.

Action Prompts

How often do you engage in creative activities such as painting, drawing, or writing? How do these activities make you feel?

_____

_____

_____

_____

_____

_____

_____

_____

_____

_____

_____

_____

Have you ever used art as a way to cope with stress or anxiety? If so, what kind of art did you engage in, and did it help?

_____

_____

_____

_____

_____

_____

_____

_____

_____

_____

_____

_____

_____

Are there any physical health conditions or symptoms that you struggle with? Have you ever tried using art or music as a way to manage these symptoms?

_____

_____

_____

_____

_____

_____

_____

_____

_____

_____

_____

_____

_____

_____

Do you enjoy listening to music? What kinds of music do you find most calming or energizing?

_____

_____

_____

_____

_____

_____

_____

_____

_____

_____

_____

_____

Have you ever participated in a dance or movement-based activity, such as yoga or tai chi? How did it make you feel?

_____

_____

_____

_____

_____

_____

_____

_____

_____

_____

_____

_____

Do you find it easy or difficult to express your thoughts and feelings? Have you ever used art as a way to express yourself?

_____

_____

_____

_____

_____

_____

_____

_____

_____

_____

_____

_____

_____

Are there any creative activities that you've always wanted to try, but haven't yet? What's holding you back?

_____

_____

_____

_____

_____

_____

_____

_____

_____

_____

_____

_____

_____

In what ways do you think engaging in creative activities could benefit your overall well-being? What steps could you take to incorporate more creativity into your life?

_____

_____

_____

_____

_____

_____

_____

_____

_____

_____

_____

_____

Amplifying Learning

Key Lessons

1. Art can enhance learning by engaging multiple parts of the brain, including sensory and emotional processing centers.

2. Integrating art into education can lead to greater retention and comprehension of information.

3. Participating in creative activities can improve critical thinking skills and encourage exploration and experimentation.

4. Collaboration and sharing of creative work can enhance communication skills and promote empathy and understanding.

5. The benefits of arts education are not limited to traditional academic subjects, but can also impact social and emotional development.

Action Prompts

Do you feel that incorporating art into your learning experiences has helped you retain information better? In what ways?

_____

_____

_____

_____

_____

_____

_____

_____

_____

_____

_____

_____

How can you integrate more creativity into your current educational or work environment?

_____

_____

_____

_____

_____

_____

_____

_____

_____

_____

_____

_____

_____

_____

_____

What kind of creative activities do you enjoy engaging in, and how can you incorporate those into your daily routine?

_____

_____

_____

_____

_____

_____

_____

_____

_____

_____

_____

_____

_____

_____

Have you ever collaborated on a creative project with others? How did the experience impact your communication and empathy skills?

_____

_____

_____

_____

_____

_____

_____

_____

_____

_____

_____

_____

Do you believe that traditional academic subjects can benefit from incorporating creative elements? Why or why not?

_____

_____

_____

_____

_____

_____

_____

_____

_____

_____

_____

_____

_____

How can you use art to explore and experiment with new ideas or concepts?

_____

_____

_____

_____

_____

_____

_____

_____

_____

_____

_____

_____

_____

_____

_____

Have you ever faced resistance or skepticism towards the integration of art in education? How did you respond to those challenges?

_____

_____

_____

_____

_____

_____

_____

_____

_____

_____

_____

_____

_____

What benefits do you think the arts have on social and emotional development? In what ways have you experienced those benefits in your own life?

_____

_____

_____

_____

_____

_____

_____

_____

_____

_____

_____

_____

_____

_____

Flourishing

Key Lessons

1. Art has the potential to enhance our sense of well-being and help us flourish by engaging our brains and bodies in unique ways.

2. Engaging in art can lead to a sense of mindfulness, or being fully present in the moment, which can help reduce stress and increase relaxation.

3. Creating art can help us build resilience by giving us a sense of control over our environment and allowing us to express our emotions in a healthy way.

4. Participating in the arts can enhance our social connections and create a sense of community and belonging.

5. Engaging with art can foster a sense of curiosity and wonder, encouraging us to explore new ideas and perspectives.

Action Prompts

How do you currently incorporate art into your life, and in what ways do you think it contributes to your overall well-being?

_____

_____

_____

_____

_____

_____

_____

_____

_____

_____

_____

_____

_____

When was the last time you fully immersed yourself in a creative activity, and how did it make you feel?

_____

_____

_____

_____

_____

_____

_____

_____

_____

_____

_____

_____

_____

_____

In what ways do you think engaging with art can help you build resilience and cope with difficult emotions?

_____

_____

_____

_____

_____

_____

_____

_____

_____

_____

_____

_____

_____

How do you feel when you share your creative work with others, and how does this contribute to your sense of community and connection?

_____

_____

_____

_____

_____

_____

_____

_____

_____

_____

_____

_____

_____

How do you think engaging with art can help you foster a sense of curiosity and wonder, and how can you incorporate this mindset into other areas of your life?

_____

_____

_____

_____

_____

_____

_____

_____

_____

_____

_____

_____

_____

How do you currently balance consuming and creating art, and do you feel like you have a healthy balance of both?

_____

_____

_____

_____

_____

_____

_____

_____

_____

_____

_____

_____

_____

_____

When you encounter art that challenges your perspectives
or beliefs, how do you respond and what can you learn
from this experience?

_____

_____

_____

_____

_____

_____

_____

_____

_____

_____

_____

_____

_____

How can you incorporate more art into your daily life, and what steps can you take to ensure that it has a positive impact on your well-being?

_____

_____

_____

_____

_____

_____

_____

_____

_____

_____

_____

_____

_____

Creating Community

Key Lessons

1. Art can bring people together and create a sense of community: Whether it's through shared experiences like going to a museum or concert, or through collaborative projects like public murals or community theater, art has the power to bring people together and foster a sense of belonging.

2. Art can help break down barriers and promote empathy: By exposing people to different perspectives and experiences, art can help them understand and empathize with others who may be different from them. This can be especially powerful in promoting diversity and inclusion.

3. Art can promote social change: Through art, people can express their views and advocate for social justice and change. This can be done through traditional forms of activism like protest art, or through more subtle forms of storytelling and narrative.

4. Art can be used as a tool for healing: Whether it's through music therapy, art therapy, or other forms

of creative expression, art can be a powerful tool for promoting emotional and physical healing.

5. Creating art together can be a bonding experience: Collaborative art projects can be a way for people to work together towards a common goal, and to build relationships and trust in the process.

Action Prompts

In what ways have you felt a sense of community through art? What specific experiences or interactions have contributed to this feeling?

_____
_____
_____
_____
_____
_____
_____
_____
_____
_____
_____
_____
_____

How has exposure to different forms of art and cultural experiences influenced your views and perspectives? Have you ever had an experience where art helped you empathize with someone from a different background or culture?

_____

_____

_____

_____

_____

_____

_____

_____

_____

_____

_____

_____

Have you ever used art as a tool for social change or activism? What specific issues or causes are important to you, and how could you use your creative skills to advocate for change?

_____

_____

_____

_____

_____

_____

_____

_____

_____

_____

_____

_____

_____

_____

Have you ever used art as a form of therapy or healing?
What specific experiences or emotions have you explored
through creative expression, and how has this impacted
your overall well-being?

_____

_____

_____

_____

_____

_____

_____

_____

_____

_____

_____

Have you ever collaborated with others on an art project? What specific skills or strengths did you bring to the project, and how did the collaborative process impact your relationship with the other participants?

_____

_____

_____

_____

_____

_____

_____

_____

_____

_____

_____

_____

_____

_____

How does art impact your overall sense of well-being and happiness? Are there specific forms of art or creative activities that you find particularly fulfilling or rejuvenating?

_____

_____

_____

_____

_____

_____

_____

_____

_____

_____

_____

_____

_____

In what ways do you think art can help bridge cultural or ideological divides? How can art be used to promote empathy and understanding between different groups of people?

_____

_____

_____

_____

_____

_____

_____

_____

_____

_____

_____

_____

_____

_____

How can you incorporate more art and creative expression into your daily life? Are there specific goals or projects you can set for yourself to help you prioritize and make time for art?

_____

_____

_____

_____

_____

_____

_____

_____

_____

_____

_____

Learning Review Questions

What made you purchase this workbook?

_____

_____

_____

_____

_____

_____

How have you been using the workbook so far?

_____

_____

_____

_____

_____

What do you feel you have gained from using the workbook?

_____

_____

_____

_____

_____

How has the workbook helped you to achieve your goals?

_____

_____

_____

_____

_____

_____

_____

Are there any parts of the workbook that were particularly helpful or challenging for you?

_____

_____

_____

_____

_____

_____

_____

How has your understanding or knowledge of the topic changed since working through the workbook?

_____

_____

_____

_____

_____

_____

_____

How do you plan to continue using the workbook or incorporating the information in your life?

_____

_____

_____

_____

_____

_____

_____

Made in the USA
Middletown, DE
22 May 2023